Bo Jackson
Baseball/Football Superstar

by Rick L. Johnson

Taking part BOOKS

dP **DILLON PRESS**
New York

Maxwell Macmillan Canada
Toronto

Maxwell Macmillan International
New York Oxford Singapore Sydney

Photographic Acknowledgments

The photographs are reproduced through the courtesy of Richard Atchison; Auburn University; the Kansas City Royals; Nike; *Seattle Times* / Alan Bergner and Harley Soltes; and Sygma / E. Adams.

Library of Congress Cataloging-in-Publication Data
Johnson, Rick L.
    Bo Jackson: Baseball / football superstar / by Rick L. Johnson.
      p. cm. — (Taking part)
    Includes index.
      Summary: A biography of the man who overcame a childhood of poverty to become one of the great stars of professional baseball and football.
    ISBN 0-87518-489-8
      1. Jackson, Bo, 1962– —Juvenile literature. 2. Baseball players—United States—Biography—Juvenile literature. Football players—United States—Biography—Juvenile literature.
      [1. Jackson, Bo, 1962– . 2. Baseball players. 3. Football players. 4. Afro-American—Biography.] I. Title II. Series.
    GV865.J28J64 1991
    796.357' 092—dc20   91-17910
    [B]

Dillon Press
Macmillan Publishing Company
866 Third Avenue
New York, NY 10022

Maxwell Macmillan Canada, Inc.
1200 Eglinton Avenue East
Suite 200
Don Mills, Ontario M3C 3N1

Macmillan Publishing Company is part of the Maxwell Communication Group of Companies.

First edition
Printed in the United States of America
10   9   8   7   6   5   4   3   2   1

About the Author

Rick L. Johnson is a free-lance writer whose articles and short stories have appeared in a variety of publications. He has coached 8- to 12-year-old baseball players and has written many articles about the sport. During his research for this book, the author interviewed Bo Jackson as well as several of his former coaches. Johnson also wrote a Taking Part biography of Jim Abbott.

Mr. Johnson has won first place for column writing and first place for sports pages in the Kansas Press Newspaper Contest. A graduate of the University of Kansas School of Journalism, he and his wife live in Concordia, Kansas.

Contents

Bo Jackson in his Kansas City Royals uniform.

Faster, Stronger, and Tougher

All of Bo Jackson's dreams were coming true. Playing baseball for the Kansas City Royals, he had made the All-Star team. Playing football for the Los Angeles Raiders, he had recently made the Pro Bowl squad. Now, in early 1991, for the first time in his pro career, his team was in a playoff game.

Early in the second half of the American Football Conference showdown against Cincinnati, Bo exploded past the line of scrimmage. As he streaked downfield, the roar of the crowd grew. Suddenly he shifted direction to avoid tacklers. Then Bengal linebacker Kevin Walker finally grabbed his legs. Jackson struggled forward before being dragged down after a thirty-four-yard run.

Bo returned to his feet, limped only a few steps toward the Raiders' sideline, then dropped back to the ground. Something was wrong with his left hip. Bo missed the rest of the game, but the injury appeared minor. It seemed he had only dislocated his hip and that it had gone back into place.

But for several weeks after the injury, Jackson failed to improve. On March 18, Royals team doctor Steve Joyce reported that he had found a small fracture in Bo's hip socket. Jackson, he said, would miss the entire 1991 baseball season.

Many doctors, after listening to Joyce's report, stated that Bo's injury could threaten his athletic career. Jackson's personal doctor, James Andrews of Birmingham, Alabama, disagreed. Andrews also had treated other sports stars, such as baseball pitcher Roger Clemens and basketball player Charles Barkley. "I really believe Bo Jackson will be back," he told

Sports Illustrated. He added that he had worked with other athletes with hip injuries similar to Bo's who had recovered.

Few people, though, expected Jackson to return to action for at least nine to twelve months. The Royals, instead of paying Jackson his full $2.375 million-a-year contract, decided to release him.

The next day, as Bo cleaned out his spring-training locker, he displayed his usual confidence. "I hope to come back to Royals Stadium and knock down the new scoreboard in left field," he told reporters.

The deep emotion he felt that day showed as he talked about leaving his friends on the Royals. He was near tears as he spoke. "If there is any hurt that comes out of this, it's because I won't be playing with my teammates—George [Brett], Sabes [Bret Saberhagen], Goobie [Mark Gubicza], Danny [Tartabull]. And I

Bo found it hard to leave his friends and teammates on the Royals.

really can't talk about the little guy, number 36 [Royals pitcher Tom Gordon], because he means so much to me."

Later in the week, Bo commented that, as a free agent, he looked forward to choosing which baseball team he would join. Then, on April 3, the Chicago White Sox announced they had signed Jackson. Bo said he had picked Chicago, in part, because he believed the team could win a World Series. The contract with the White Sox allowed him to play for the Raiders once he recovered from his injury.

Everyone knew that before a return to his two-sport career, Jackson faced a long struggle. But that did not frighten Bo. He could clearly remember all of the hard battles he had already won in his life. Many of them happened years before.

As a small child, Vincent Jackson knew who other children's favorite "Sesame Street" characters were. Some liked Big Bird the most. Others liked Ernie. But neither was his choice. His favorite was Oscar the Grouch.

Oscar lived in a garbage can, and Vincent's home was just as cramped. His mother and eight of his nine brothers and sisters lived near Bessemer, Alabama, in a three-room house. The only bedroom had just two beds, so Vincent usually slept on the floor.

Like Oscar, Vincent could yell and look mean. Sometimes he was so difficult to deal with that he reminded his family of a wild boar hog. They shortened "Boar" to "Bo," and that became his nickname.

In grade school Bo often fought with other children. He stuttered when he spoke, so it was hard for him to read out loud in class. Whenever someone laughed at his stutter, he would start a fight with that person after school. Bo never lost those fights.

Soon he became a bully and began ordering other

children to give him their lunch money or he would beat them up. Even those children two or three grades above Bo were afraid of him.

Florence Jackson Bond tried hard to make her son behave. Bo, born in Bessemer on November 30, 1962, was the eighth of her ten children. None of the others caused so much trouble. Bo stole from her own purse, and he even hit his female cousins.

"If you don't change your ways," she told him over and over, "you're going to be in jail." Her warnings, though, did not stop his stealing and fighting.

She tried punishing him by forcing him to do extra chores. She would wake him before the sun came up to make him take out the garbage or do yard work. Sometimes she whipped him when he was bad. But nothing she did made Bo listen to her.

Florence Bond had other concerns, too. She worked hard as a motel maid, but providing enough food for such a large family was difficult. Bo's father lived on the other side of Bessemer and worked in a steel mill. Often it was months between the times Bo saw him.

Aunts and uncles and cousins, though, were a part of many of the fun family times. On some fall Saturdays his uncle would kill a hog and they would have a family feast. Sometimes his brothers and sisters and cousins had crab apple battles. Everyone wanted to be on Bo's side because he could throw so well.

Bo also could run fast. Once, in the third grade, he saw the fourth, fifth, and sixth grade classes practicing track. He joined them and outran everybody. The coach asked him to be on the team, and he won two races at his first track meet.

Even in grade school, according to Bo, "I didn't take too kindly to someone being faster than I was." That included his friends.

"I was not going to let any of the other kids outdo me at anything—fighting, throwing rocks, swimming— anything. I always put it upon myself to be faster, stronger, and tougher than all my other buddies."

As a baseball player, he soon became *too* good to play on a team with his friends. He had joined a Little League squad when he was ten years old and played catcher. But after only a few weeks, the coaches said he was too rough for that age level. They moved him up to the Pony League, where he caught and pitched against thirteen- and fourteen-year-olds.

When he pitched, he struck out most batters. His fielders were so sure of him that, for the last out of the game, they tossed their gloves off. As they sat on the ground and cheered, Bo would strike out the final batter.

In addition to sports, Bo enjoyed riding bicycles. "My friends and I were bicycle wizards," said Bo.

"We'd find an old bike at the city dump and take it home and within two hours we'd have it fixed up and back on the road."

One summer, when Bo was thirteen, he and his friends found themselves in deep trouble. On their daily walk to a swimming hole, they always passed a pen full of pigs. Sometimes they stopped to throw rocks at the pigs or to beat them with sticks. They even killed some of them.

One day a person who worked on the farm spotted Bo and his friends pounding on a large hog with sticks. "Hey! Get out of here!" the man shouted.

Bo leapt over the pigpen fence, soared across a wide ditch, and raced for home. He had been able to outrun trouble before, and he hoped he could again. But soon there was a knock on the door. The man who chased them out of the pen had recognized Bo.

Florence Bond listened as the farmer described

what had happened. Bo and his friends, he said, had killed almost $3,000 worth of his boss's pigs.

"If the man who owns the pigs wants to send him to reform school, then send him, 'cause I'm tired of his ways," she said. "I can't do nothin' with him."

She turned toward Bo, and he could tell how serious she was. He was scared. This time trouble had caught up with him.

In high school, Bo Jackson starred in baseball and other sports.

I Started to Grow Up

Some days Bo woke up feeling mean. Perhaps he was angry because he had no father in his home, or because his family was poor. Whatever the reason, sometimes he wanted to strike out at the whole world.

To help pay for the pigs he had killed, Bo mowed lawns and did other chores. That kept him out of reform school—this time. But he was afraid of what might happen the next time he could not control the anger he felt inside.

Bo wanted to go to college someday. First, though, he knew that he had to learn to manage his temper. His high school football and track coach, Dick Atchison, helped him discover a way to do that.

If he could hold his temper until after school,

Dick Atchison, Bo Jack-son's high school football and track coach.

Coach Atchison told Bo, then he could let it go during practice. The coach taught him to take his meanness out on running and jumping. Bo quickly showed Coach Atchison his track skills. As a freshman at McAdory High School, he finished tenth in the decathlon at the Alabama state meet. In a decathlon contest, athletes perform in ten different track events.

"I loved to high jump," Bo said. "That's really where I got rid of all my anger—jumping as high as I could."

During high school, Bo sensed himself changing. "I started to grow up," Bo later recalled in his autobiography, *Bo Knows Bo.* "I didn't go out looking for trouble."

Instead, after practice he went home and studied. He had been held back in first grade because of his stutter, not because he wasn't smart. In high school he received good grades, and he really liked science and English.

On the athletic field, Bo kept improving. As a sophomore, he became a starting running back for the varsity football team.

Despite his success, Bo's mom wanted him to quit football. Afraid he would be hurt, she told him, "Don't stay at school and practice or I'm going to lock you out." And sometimes she would.

But instead of quitting football, whenever his mom locked the door on him, he went to a friend's house. Bo thought that earning a football scholarship might be a way for him to continue his education after high school. His family now lived in a bigger home, but he knew that there wouldn't be enough money to send him to college.

Sometimes the lack of his mom's complete support for his interest in sports frustrated him. He tried to convince her that he could win an athletic scholarship—and that he was growing up. During the summer he worked at a recreation center near his home. Now, instead of causing trouble there as he once did, he watched younger children to make sure they behaved.

As a junior Bo starred in three sports for McAdory High in McCalla, Alabama, a small town near Bo's home. In football that year, he rushed for eight hundred yards, and in track he won the state decathlon title. In baseball he batted .432 and as a pitcher won nine games and lost only one.

By Bo's senior year, he had grown to six feet, one inch and weighed 205 pounds. Finally his mom

Bo and his teammates on the football team posed for this picture in the McAdory High School yearbook. Bo is number 40 in the back row.

began to worry less about his hurting himself playing football. Then, according to Bo, she backed his athletic goals "one hundred percent."

That fall he rushed for 1,173 yards, averaging almost 11 yards per carry from his fullback position. He also played defensive end and kicked for McAdory. He took pride in his all-around skills. One of his favorite moments came during a homecoming game.

"We were ahead of a high school named Dora

about 32-0 at the half," said Bo. "I had scored all the touchdowns and kicked the field goals and the extra points, so the announcer said, 'Your halftime score: Bo Jackson 32, Dora 0.'"

With each outstanding game, his dream of receiving a college scholarship grew closer. Meanwhile, McAdory teachers such as baseball coach Terry Brasseale watched Bo continue to mature off the field.

Through his early high school years, Bo hadn't seemed interested in making new friends. "In twelfth grade he changed," Brasseale said. "He started being real nice to everybody—talkative. I think he became more aware of what he could be."

When Bo was a senior at McAdory, he was not voted best student-athlete. However, he did show how much he had grown up. The winner of the award was teammate Steve Mann, the quarterback on the football team and a pitcher on the baseball team.

Because Mann was white, angry black students at the school wondered if his race was the reason he received the honor. At a meeting between the principal and the school's seniors, black and white students exchanged heated words. Black students said they would refuse to attend class unless Bo was given the award. Loud voices, growing even more furious, filled the usually quiet library. Then Bo stood up. Suddenly the room was silent as they waited for him to speak.

"Look, I'm not here to get any awards," he said. "I'm here to get an education. You can all stay here and fight or argue, whatever you want to do, but I'm going back to class."

Soon the seniors realized that fighting over an award was senseless. Anyway, according to Bo, his classmate probably did deserve the honor. Mann was a good athlete, too. And although his own grades were good, Bo knew Steve's were better.

Bo at bat during a high school baseball game.

After his busy spring season, Bo's decision about college grew more difficult. As expected, he defended his state decathlon title, but his outstanding play in baseball drew the attention of professional teams.

In only twenty-five games, he hit twenty home runs to tie the national high school single-season record. The New York Yankees offered him $250,000 if he would sign with them.

Bo, unsure what to do, thought of all the people

who had guided him while he was growing up. His older brothers and sisters had often provided him with their advice. His Aunt Bea had always been helpful when the family needed her. And of course his coaches had been important to him.

One person, though, had influenced Bo's life more than any other—his mom. He loved and respected her very much, even though it was hard for him to say that to her. Before making his decision, he asked for her advice.

"You go to college," Florence Bond told him. "You can have money for a short time, but education is for your whole life."

So many times in the past Bo had disagreed with her, often refusing to even listen. Now, although old enough to do as he pleased, he carefully considered her words. And this time Bo agreed with his mom.

Bo Jackson of Auburn

Bo took the pitch from Auburn University quarterback Randy Campbell and raced toward the left sideline. He sensed the Alabama Crimson Tide defense rolling toward him, preparing to smother him.

As he looked upfield, though, he spotted an opening. He quickly cut toward that hole and burst between the defenders. Once past them, he sprinted toward the goal line, avoiding other tacklers until he reached the thirteen-yard line.

A few plays later, the Auburn Tigers kicked a field goal to cut the lead against their state rivals, 22 to 17. Auburn still had a chance to end its nine-game losing streak to the University of Alabama.

Perhaps Bo had never wanted so much to win a

At Auburn University, Bo Jackson won the Heisman Trophy as the nation's best college football player.

game. Earlier in the year, Alabama had lost the recruiting battle to sign Bo. Shortly after that, a Crimson Tide coach said that Bo Jackson could look forward to losing to Alabama for four years. Through high school, sports had seemed so easy for Bo that there were times he almost grew bored with them. A challenge like the one the Alabama coach had set before him made athletics much more interesting.

Now, whether or not he met that challenge would be decided on one play. It was fourth down and goal for Auburn at the one-yard line. With less than three minutes left in the game, the Tigers needed a touchdown to win.

"Play 43," the quarterback called.

Bo took the handoff and thrust himself high over the linemen, determined to land in the end zone. In midair a defender blocked his path, but he stretched his body forward as far as he could. Down the line he

Bo Jackson leaps high over the goal line for an Auburn touchdown.

spotted the official, who gave the signal he wanted to see—Auburn touchdown!

Jackson finished with 114 yards rushing and received the game's Most Valuable Player award. With his football talents thrilling large crowds and with his stutter improving, Bo's confidence in himself continued to grow.

After the football season, he showed his rare all-around athletic skills by winning letters in both track and baseball. That made him the first Southeastern Conference athlete in twenty years to be a three-sport letterman.

Because of his other sports, Bo always missed spring football practice. However, as a sophomore he took part in Auburn's annual football scrimmage in a different way—racing against children.

"Bo Jackson had the idea himself," said Auburn's sports information director, David Housel. Before the scrimmage, Bo would give anyone who wanted to race him down the football field a lead of about fifteen yards. If someone beat him, he promised to buy them dinner.

That day several hundred children lined up in front of Bo. "On your mark!" the public address announcer called. "Get set!" Suddenly, all of the boys and girls broke for the goal line, adding even more to their lead. "Go!" Finally, Bo started after them.

He raced past them all, but there were no sad losers. The rest of the evening, Jackson signed autographs for everyone. "Bo wants kids to know that older people love and care about them," said Housel.

Bo's major was family and child development. One reason he had decided to attend Auburn was Pat Dye, the school's football coach. Dye had been honest with Bo, telling him he would have to earn his position on the football field. The only thing that he

After he became a professional sports star, Bo returned to an Auburn football game with his two sons, Garrett and Nicholas.

could promise Bo, Dye said, was that Auburn could give him a good education. But that, too, Bo knew he would have to earn with his own hard work.

Bo especially enjoyed the time he spent at Auburn's Child Development Center. There, as part of his studies, he taught and played with children.

"He has a real concern for children as people," a teacher at the center, Janice Grover, told *People* magazine. "He makes it a point to get down to their eye level to talk to them."

Sometimes Bo visited area schools to speak to children about avoiding drugs. "I get high off of nature, sports, and being around kids," he said.

Bo's best friends included teammates Lionel James, Tommie Agee, and Tim Jessie. They enjoyed picking up food at a restaurant and then going fishing. Once Tim, casting his fishing lure toward the lake, accidentally caught the fishhook in Bo's head.

Luckily, the injury wasn't serious. At the hospital, even the doctor laughed when he saw the hook sticking from the head of Auburn's star player. It seemed, reported the newspaper the next day, that Tim Jessie had caught a world-record bass.

A much more serious injury during Jackson's junior year forced him to miss half of the football season. In the second game of 1984, against the University of Texas, Jackson separated his right shoulder. During his recovery, Bo spent time studying with a classmate in his child development courses, Linda Garrett. The friendship bloomed into romance, and three years later they would marry.

Also as a junior, Jackson decided to skip track to focus on baseball. That spring he hit .401 and played center field for Auburn. His outstanding season caused debate about whether he would become a pro football or pro baseball player.

First, though, Bo had another goal. Since his freshman year at Auburn, he had dreamed of winning the Heisman Trophy. His senior season would be his last chance to earn that award, which each year goes to the nation's best college football player.

Jackson opened the 1985 season by gaining a career high 290 yards in a 49–7 victory against Southwestern Louisiana. Nothing, it seemed, would keep him from his goal.

However, injuries slowed him down during three of Auburn's eleven regular season games. Although he still finished with a school record 1,786 rushing yards, Bo knew that other players were also strong Heisman candidates. Iowa quarterback Chuck Long, Michigan State tailback Lorenzo White, and Miami quarterback Vinny Testaverde also had great seasons.

Jackson usually didn't consider awards important. Two years before, when Auburn defeated the

Bo Jackson gave the Most Valuable Player trophy from the Sugar Bowl game to his teammate Lionel James.

University of Michigan in the Sugar Bowl, he was named the game's Most Valuable Player. But he gave the trophy to teammate Lionel James, saying his friend deserved the honor.

The Heisman Trophy, though, was a special award Bo wanted very much to win. It would mean he had reached the top after starting his life at what most people would consider the very bottom.

He never complained, however, about the hurdles he had faced. Bo knew the struggles had made him a stronger person. He would not wish for other children to endure similar problems. But if his own childhood had been easier, he doubted he would be a Heisman Trophy candidate.

On December 7, Bo sat beside the other leading candidates in New York's Downtown Athletic Club. Football fans across the nation watched the televised broadcast, eager to hear who the 1985 Heisman winner would be.

"In the closest vote in the history of this trophy"— the announcer paused, and Bo felt as if everyone around him could hear his throbbing heart—"Bo Jackson of Auburn."

Bo Jackson surprised everyone when he chose to play professional baseball for the Kansas City Royals instead of professional football.

Everybody Doubted Bo but Bo

The Tampa Bay Buccaneers would have to pay more than four million dollars to sign Heisman Trophy winner Bo Jackson. National Football League experts predicted greatness for the nation's number one draft choice. They compared Jackson to past football legends. "He's like O. J. Simpson . . . only bigger and stronger," said one NFL general manager.

The chance of a baseball career now seemed slim. No major league team could offer an unproven baseball player the high salary that a Heisman Trophy winner could command. The Kansas City Royals waited until the fourth round to pick Jackson. They didn't want to waste one of their high draft picks on someone likely to choose football.

Money, though, would not be the only factor in Jackson's decision. He announced his choice on June 21, 1986, in Birmingham, Alabama.

"When you've been playing both sports for six or seven years and just decide to give one up to concentrate on one, it's really hard," Bo said. "I have made that decision. I have chosen baseball over football."

Some reporters thought that Kansas City must have matched Tampa Bay's huge contract offer. But the Royals offer was many times less than that of the Buccaneers.

According to Jackson's agent, Richard Woods, "He did what he wanted to do and turned his back on millions and millions of dollars. It's hard to believe, I know. You have to know Bo Jackson to understand how something like this could happen."

Jackson explained that he loved baseball and that he chose "what's in my heart." He also seemed ready for a new challenge. "I'm not trying to brag, but I got my [football] trophy," he said.

In addition, the risk of injury is greater in football, and baseball players' careers usually last longer. So, in the long run, he might earn more money playing baseball.

But that was *if* his talent could carry him to the major leagues. Many powerful sluggers never learned to hit a curveball. One reporter pointed out that Bo had batted only .246 during his final season at Auburn.

"In life you take chances," Bo said of his choice.

Baseball experts predicted that it would take two to three years for Jackson to become a regular in the major leagues. How would he feel about playing in the minor leagues?

"I'm so happy right now," Bo answered, "I wouldn't care if they sent me to the Pee Wee League."

Jackson played his first professional game on June 30 for the Memphis Chicks, a Royals minor league team. The game attracted 7,026 fans, more than twice the normal crowd. In his first at bat, Bo grounded a single up the middle. Excited fans gave him a standing ovation.

But Bo struggled through his first twelve games. After forty-five at bats he had only four hits for a .089 average. He was learning, though, and by September he had raised his average to .277.

During the off-season Jackson spent two weeks in the Florida Instructional League before returning to Auburn. There he presented Linda with an engagement ring. They would be married on September 5.

"She's my transmission. Without her, my car can't run," Bo said. "I can talk to her about anything."

Linda was always eager to hear Bo's thoughts. "He'd watch and study and check things out for

Bo swings hard during a Royals game.

months and then share his observations," Linda told Dick Schaap, the coauthor of Bo's autobiography. "He didn't come to hasty decisions. I was amazed by how wise he was."

The biggest challenge for Bo, she believed, was dealing with all the attention a star athlete receives. Always, it seemed, reporters and fans wanted to know more about his personal life. The on-the-field challenges, though, she knew he could handle.

In the Royals 1987 spring-training camp, Bo's hard work pleased Kansas City general manager John Schuerholz. "I never expected anybody could make the kind of strides toward improvement that he has made," said Schuerholz.

On the weekend before the season opener, Jackson's batting average was .290, and he led the team in runs batted in. That Saturday he learned he would start in left field for the Royals on opening day.

Schuerholz told Jackson he hoped Bo could help Kansas City win 110 games, which would be a fantastic season.

"Let's make it 130," a confident Bo told him.

In an early season game against the Detroit Tigers, nothing seemed out of Jackson's reach. He already had three hits, including a three-run homer, when he came to bat in the sixth inning.

With the bases loaded, Detroit relief pitcher Nate Snell threw a slider that broke about three inches outside the plate. Bo swung, and as he connected with the ball, he heard his bat crack.

Bo trotted toward first base, expecting a Tiger outfielder to catch the drive toward right-center field. After all, he had not made good contact. But the baseball kept soaring, and it finally landed in the Royals Stadium waterfall for a grand slam home run.

Although the broken-bat home run surprised Bo,

his overall play did not. "Everybody doubted Bo but Bo," he told reporters after the game. "I like to make a liar out of people who doubt me."

Kansas City hitting coach Hal McRae was impressed by more than Jackson's strength. "He's got the greatest bat speed I've ever seen, and lifting his front leg is one of the many good things he does naturally."

The Royals knew, though, that their young player would have many ups and downs. Consistent play, McRae said, is something that comes with a lot of painful trials and errors. Only four days after his four-hit night, Bo struck out five times in one game against the New York Yankees.

Near the midway point of the season, Jackson already had eighteen home runs and forty-five runs batted in. Then, at a July news conference in Toronto, he again surprised the sports world. In addition to

After much practice and hard work, Bo became a professional baseball star.

playing baseball for the Royals, he said, he hoped to play football for the Los Angeles Raiders. The NFL team had agreed to let Jackson make football a part-time career.

"I have to do my job with the Kansas City Royals before I do anything else," Bo said. "Whatever comes after the baseball season is a hobby for Bo Jackson—just like fishing and hunting."

Once again doubters surrounded Bo. Many people said no one could be a success at two professional sports at the same time. It had been decades since anyone had tried it for more than two years.

Even Jim Thorpe had not fully succeeded. Thorpe, an American Indian, showed his athletic ability when he won the decathlon at the 1912 Olympics. He then became a star pro football player but found pro baseball difficult. He hit only .252 with just seven home runs during six seasons in the major leagues.

Bo Jackson, according to critics, was foolish to attempt what no one had been able to do.

The man who loved challenges now faced his biggest ever.

Playing for the Los Angeles Raiders, Bo Jackson runs past a tackler.

That Was Fun

A nationwide "Monday Night Football" audience watched Bo Jackson celebrate his twenty-fifth birthday. It was a night for both Bo and pro football fans to remember.

Playing in only his fifth contest for the Los Angeles Raiders, he broke the team's single-game rushing record. Included in his 221-yard performance against the Seattle Seahawks was a thrilling 91-yard touchdown run.

Even Bo Jackson critics were impressed, but their question remained. Could he survive the grind of playing both sports for more than a year or two?

After the football season, he would have no more than six to eight weeks off in January and February.

Then it would be time to begin spring training with the Royals. Once the baseball season ended in October, he would take only a few days off before joining the Raiders.

Jackson's third year of following that routine began in 1989, and he showed no signs of wearing down.

During the first half of the baseball season, he made an amazing play that became known simply as "The Throw." With Seattle's speedy Harold Reynolds racing around third base, Jackson fielded the ball off the outfield fence. He whirled and launched a three hundred-foot strike to home plate to throw out Reynolds.

In July he led off the All-Star Game with a towering 448-foot home run. Later he added a single and a stolen base and accepted the game's Most Valuable Player trophy.

As he gained experience, Bo played well as an outfielder as well as a batter.

Even baseball's stars talked about Jackson as though he was their hero. Royals veteran second baseman Frank White knew tales of Bo's feats would continue far into the future. "I can't wait to tell my grandkids one day that I played with Bo Jackson," White commented. "They won't believe it."

In November 1989, in a football game against the Cincinnati Bengals, Jackson scored on a ninety-two-yard run. That play, along with Bo's ninety-one-yard run in 1987, set a National Football League record. Never before had an NFL player broken loose for two touchdown runs of ninety or more yards.

Jackson's combination of speed and strength drew praise from other pro football stars. "Very possibly," said Bengals quarterback Boomer Esiason, "you're looking at the finest athlete this country has seen in the last fifty years."

Suddenly Bo Jackson critics were silent. The explosions off his powerful bat and the roar of the crowd on his touchdown runs had drowned out their words. For three years Bo had not simply played pro football and baseball—he had become a *star* in both sports!

His success continued during 1990. After hitting

twenty-eight home runs and batting .272 for the Royals, he helped the Raiders to the AFC West title. Then came the January 13 playoff game in which Jackson badly hurt his hip. The early portion of his recovery program included exercising in a swimming pool and bicycling. "When I come back, watch out," Bo said.

In addition to working his way back from a serious injury, other challenges remained for Bo, too. The most important ones to him were those he faced as a husband and father. He and Linda have three children. Their sons, Garrett and Nicholas, were joined by a daughter, Morgan, in July 1990.

Linda is proud of Bo for more than his athletic achievements. In Kansas City she worked at the Marillac Center, which treats children for sexual and physical abuse. Bo also was involved with the center. Sometimes, according to Linda, children who have

Linda and Bo Jackson with their three children: Garrett, Nicholas, and Morgan.

withdrawn from everyone else will respond to Bo.

"They don't talk about his home runs or touch-downs," she said. "They talk about how he pushes them on the swings or holds their hands or plays catch with them."

Linda has her master's degree in counseling psychology from Auburn. She is partway toward her doctorate degree in child psychology. Bo is just four courses short of his family and child development degree.

While Bo played for the Royals, they owned a two-story rock home in Leawood, Kansas, a suburb of Kansas City. Surrounded by a well-kept yard, the house included a weight room, sauna, and library.

The family rents a home in Los Angeles while Bo plays for the Raiders. There are both bad and good things about living in California. The earthquakes worry Bo. However, he and his family have enjoyed meeting superstars such as singer Michael Jackson and basketball player Magic Johnson.

Bo, Linda, and their children return to Alabama about twice each year. There they visit his mother, other relatives, his father, and friends from high school and college.

According to Linda, the intense nature he shows on the athletic field usually isn't present at other times.

"When I leave the ballpark," Bo explained, "I leave everything there. When I hit the driveway, I become a husband and father."

In his spare time, Bo enjoys the outdoors, from simply walking in the woods to hunting and fishing. His marksmanship with a rifle helped him win the 1989 Buckmasters, a deer-hunting contest in Alabama. Archery also is a favorite pastime, and observers say he has great skill at shooting a bow and arrow.

Bo Jackson carries a surfboard in this "Bo Family Reunion" commercial.

Everyone knows that even Bo cannot do everything, but sometimes it does seem as if he can. The idea that Bo has talents in many fields has been used in commercials that feature him. He is a spokesperson for Nike, Pepsi-Cola, AT&T, and other companies.

Jackson displays the same style and flair in his commercials that he does on the football and baseball field. His excitement for everything that he does is attractive to fans. Bo, after a thrilling game, has joyfully declared to reporters, "That was fun, real fun."

But perhaps the most obvious Bo Jackson trait is the strength he shows in following his own path. No one—not the public, not his teammates, and not the owners—seems to control his decisions.

The reasons for Bo's success, though, go far beyond that quality. After all, as a child he often went his own direction, doing whatever he pleased. Then, however, it usually led him nowhere.

Understanding right from wrong, discovering his own goals, and building total confidence—all have been necessary steps to his success.

And Bo is not one to forget the lessons he learned and the hard road he traveled before he became famous. In an instant he can recall those winter nights on a cold floor. Then, in the struggle to keep warm, he slept so close to the heater that he sometimes burned himself.

Now Bo's own children have a warm home and more toys than he could have dreamed of as a child. But he also wants to give them something more.

He wants to teach them everything that his mom taught him.

No doubt, that is another goal Bo Jackson will reach.

Achievements

1981 Set Alabama high school Class 3A triple jump record (48-7 1/4).

1982 Set Alabama high school Class 3A 100-yard dash record (9.59).

1982 Tied national high school single-season home run record (20).

1985 Received Southland Olympia Award for outstanding amateur athletic performance.

1985 Set Auburn University career rushing record (4,303 yards).

1985 Set Auburn University career touchdown record (44).

1985 Won Heisman Trophy.

1987 Set Kansas City Royals rookie home run record (22).

1987 Broke Los Angeles Raiders single-game rushing record (221 yards).

1987 Named to National Football League All-Rookie team.

1989 Led American League All-Star balloting (received 1,748,696 votes from fans).

1989 Picked as All-Star Game Most Valuable Player.

1989 Selected as leftfielder on *USA Today* All-1989 team.

1990 Named to American Football Conference Pro Bowl squad.

For the Kansas City Royals

Year	G	AB	R	H	Avg.	HR	RBI	SB	SO
1986	25	82	9	17	.207	2	9	3	34
1987	116	396	46	93	.235	22	52	10	159
1988	124	439	63	108	.246	25	68	27	146
1989	135	515	86	132	.256	32	105	26	172
1990	111	405	74	110	.272	28	78	15	128
Total	511	1,837	278	460	.250	109	312	81	639

G: games   HR: home runs
AB: at bats   RBI: runs batted in
R: runs scored   SB: stolen bases
H: hits   SO: strikeouts
Avg.: batting average

For the Los Angeles Raiders

		Rushing					Receiving		
Year	G	Att.	Yds.	Avg.	TD	No.	Yds.	Avg.	TD
1987	7	81	554	6.8	4	16	136	8.5	2
1988	10	136	580	4.3	3	9	79	8.7	0
1989	11	173	950	5.5	4	9	69	7.7	0
1990	10	125	698	5.6	5	6	68	11.3	0
Total	38	515	2,782	5.4	16	40	352	8.8	2

G: games   Avg.: average yards gained
Att.: attempts rushing   TD: touchdowns
Yds.: yards gained   No.: number of passes caught

Index